what matters

ISBN 13: 978-1-105-16235-0

Printed in the United States of America
First Printing: 2011
14   13   12   11   10   5   4   3   2   1

Cover and interior designs by Emsster Design Company

what matters
... gratitude

MISSY DURANT

wnat matters

... gratitude

For Sam and our children,
Thing 1 and Thing, Thing 1

This is my story: a lifetime of moments, a pile of letters, and an unwavering gratitude for life, itself. I tell you this story to honor all the people in my life who have either told me a story or been a part of my story. Those who shared their stories with me created a place for me to live—a place to dream and fail and learn. I tell you this story with the hope that it will inspire you to listen, to own your story, to honor the people in your own life, and that it will give you a chance to answer this question:

What Matters?

CHAPTER 1
Grab Your Life

Never waste a good crisis.

The last five words mentioned in passing from a colleague when I stepped out of the corporate world in 2009.

I am toe to toe with mid-life and I have a choice. I can have an affair or buy a fast red car. But those last five words continue to govern my thoughts.

Never waste a good crisis.

Instead, I'll start searching the cobwebbed memories of my past for the answer. An answer to a question I am embarrassed to say I've lost.

What matters?

Part of my answer is in the black, tattered roller bag I've been dragging around for years. It is filled with good intent. The weight of this bag has been bearable...until now.

Now, I am standing at an intersection in life, when looking forward and back have meaning. I need to unpack and sort through my messy life for an answer. Maybe an answer will unfold if I stop and

remember the people and moments in my life that made a difference. Maybe all I need to do is stop and listen.

Never waste a good crisis.

This is an invitation to dive into your own moments and swim
in gratitude.

Grab your life and come with me.

CHAPTER 2
THE YELLOW ROOM

February 8, 2009, was a Sunday. It was a Sunday like any other. Sitting on the sofa, mindlessly scanning Facebook, I noticed a post from an old classmate. Our high school American Literature teacher, Ms. Miller, had passed away. Memories flooded my mind.

+ + + + + +

I'm sixteen and in love, and I share the moment of my first kiss with no one. Summer love. Falling in love for the first time is magical. Every cell in my teenage body is alive. Love beams from my body, and the topic of my new love oozes into every conversation I have with my friends. It all feels like a fairytale to me. But the fairytale ending was not meant to be.

My love is a secret. Because everyone—*everyone* I know—says it is bad. It is wrong and not something I can talk about. It scares me sometimes to think about it. I will go to hell for sure if—no, *when*—they find out. And they will find out, I know.

I share the moment of my first kiss with no one. I hold this moment as tight as I can, replaying it over and over in my mind. I tell myself that sharing the story of my kiss would be a fatal error, reputation suicide, and just plain stupid for a teenager in a small town in the South. My parents will be ridiculed.

I kissed a girl. I fell in love with a girl. And a girl broke my heart.

"It will be the best thing for you," she said. The words echoed, getting louder and louder. Her parents are Southern Baptist—the kind that save the lost. I know this because they saved me at thirteen, even though I wasn't lost. Now there is a sinner in the family and she must be saved.

"No, no. It will be fine," she says. My heart begins to feel the pain of love being ripped away for the first time.

"But, I love you," I plead.

She shakes her head. It is over.

+ + + + + +

A week passes. A girl broke my heart and I can't tell anyone, because she was my best friend. I'm drowning and I can't yell for help. I am sinking beneath the weight of a broken heart.

Now I am walking down the hallway on the beige linoleum floor leading toward the back of my ranch style house. My golden retriever, Harmony, follows me with her tail wagging, always happy to see me. There are three bedrooms at the end of the hall, one on the right, one on the left, and one straight ahead.

I turn right into my parents' room and walk straight to the nightstand on my dad's side of the bed. I open the drawer of his nightstand and pause, wondering why my dad chose this to keep when his mom died. Why would he keep a gun? I wonder if he's ever fired it. I reach in, take it out, and walk back out into the hall.

I turn into my room.

"Close the door," I say to myself, even though no one is home. I close it for a reason.

There are two twin beds pushed together, a luxury I have because my older sister is in college. The room is yellow, not bright and not pale, just yellow. It's late in the afternoon, so the sun has moved to the front of the house, coloring the yellow flowered curtains darker than normal. I walk across the room and sit on the side of the bed. The comforter is the same pattern as the curtains. I stare at the yellow painted desk across from the bed.

Time slows.

We picked these out with the yellow stamps I won at a drawing at Winn Dixie. Smiling, I remember when my sister and I made the trip to the yellow stamp reward store and picked the bedding set. It seems a lifetime ago, but it was only a couple of years. It seemed important at the time.

Now it will have another purpose.

"Why? Why do I have to be different?" I ask aloud. I'm feeling overwhelmed and panicky. "Gay—why me?!" I scream. No one will hear me.

The gun feels heavy in my hand. The barrel is short, oily, and smells like old metal. I've never held a gun before. The grip is small—the perfect size for my hand. I can feel the roughness of the plastic press into my palm. I switch the gun to my left hand and see the brass ends of the bullets in the cylinder.

It will be over soon.

I switch the gun back to my right hand and squeeze the gun tighter. I can feel my heartbeat pulsing in my hand against the handle, slick with sweat. I hold the muzzle closer to my face and close my eyes, squeezing out tears. The smell of metal is overwhelming. I feel there is no other option but killing the sadness in a split second, because I found and lost love in a split second. I am hopeless.

I can feel the small ridges of the plastic grip pushing deeper into my sweaty palm. The grip is there for a reason.

I hear my heart beating, feel my body shaking.

"No." I open my eyes.

I lay the gun on the bed, the gray metal a stark contrast on the yellow flowered bedspread. A wave of strength washes over me. It came from nowhere and everywhere. The strength pushes me forward in time. I have no idea why I don't pull the trigger. I just don't.

"No," I say out loud again as I walk towards the door with the gun in my hand, pointed at the floor. In the same number of steps it took to get the gun, I put it back in the drawer. Back in the hall, I slide down next to Harmony, whose tail makes a comforting rhythmic sound on the floor. Thump, thump, thump. I look at my dog, the only other being in the world who knows what just happened.

Both of my secrets are safe.

Being gay will be an asterisk in my life, I decide, but not my whole life. I will pull myself up by my bootstraps, just like my mom. From this moment on, I will do everything possible to achieve, to lead, to exceed even the most unreasonable expectations. I will become a master of conversational diversion, and my accomplishments will be all I will need to survive. Overachieving will be the perfect way to distract anyone who asks about my personal life. It's a logical solution to overcome the one thing that makes me different.

The perfect cover.

+ + + + + + +

Two months later, school starts and so does my overachieving. As always, it's hot, which certainly isn't helping my nerves. I walk in the side door of the classroom. I hear my heart pumping a familiar song of fear.

I can do this.

Ms. Miller is sitting at her desk. A desk covered in papers, neatly scattered, most of which have notes with her intense, focused handwriting in the only pen she uses—a black felt tipped. It's the same pen she rolls between her hands every day during class, making a rhythmic sound when it moves back and forth over her rings.

Clack-clack, clack-clack, clack-clack.

Ms. Miller looks at me and smiles. It is the kind of reassuring smile that a teacher gives when she senses that a child is afraid. Still she waits for me to speak, somehow knowing the courage it takes to speak is part of the process.

"I really want to be in your class. I tried talking to my counselor, and, well, she doesn't think I'd do well in here. She said the class is full."

Ms. Miller looks over her glasses and waits for me to continue.

"I want to go to college. Everyone knows that if you get into this class and learn to write a term paper, you have a better chance of getting into a good college. I want to go to FSU."

She looks at me with her intense, dark eyes through her small, black, oval rimmed glasses, sizing me up. After a lifetime of minutes, she finally says, "There's one chair left in the back. Take that one." Then as if nothing different has occurred, she walks to the back of the room, perches on her stool, and begins the class.

By the end of class, I am looking at a list of American authors, and I don't recognize any of the names.

"Which one are you going to pick?"

I am caught off guard by Ms. Miller's question and blurt, "Gertrude Stein!" *God, I hope that's the right answer. Maybe she'll walk away now. Please be the right answer, please. I need this class.*

"I think you'll like that one," she says. The look in her eyes is knowing and certain.

+ + + + + + +

Ms. Miller was the only teacher who taught from the back of the classroom, poised intently on her stool, inspiring us to learn. She placed all of the responsibility for learning on each student by asking questions, expecting us to use our minds and search for an answer, instead of lecturing at us. She was a mentor—a modern day Willa Cather. She brought the concepts of inequality, respect, and tolerance to life through the characters in the American classic novel, *To Kill a Mockingbird*. Her dog-eared copy was as much an artifact of the years of use as it was a compass for her own actions. She shared the same courage as Atticus' Finch. Both believed in people, especially those that others found dismissible.

Literature was her life. Words were her life. When she read Walt Whitman's poem, *I Sing the Body Electric*, each word would hang in the air until the phrase ended, then flow into our sponge-like minds, challenging us to think. Her room was a classroom of transformation, into which kids casually sauntered in, at the beginning of the year and young adults confidently strode out, by the year's end. She bred success in every student, setting high, yet reasonable, expectations for us all.

When Ms. Miller gave me a seat in her class, it changed my life.

In that moment, she taught me that rules are made for natural disasters and emergencies, and the rest of the time they are guidelines that help us make decisions. She gave me the gift of a role model with Gertrude Stein, a writer from another time and a silent beacon of hope during my turbulent teenage years. Ms. Miller was a teacher and a woman who made a difference in the lives of many students. In one moment, Carlene Miller changed the course of my life.

A difference that would last a lifetime.

+ + + + + + +

Now sitting on the couch that Sunday in 2009, I suddenly feel a huge sense of regret that I never told her what a difference she made in my life. Regret so heavy, I can feel my body begin to sink from the weight. I have no idea what to do next but feel the depth of regret. I know I have a choice. I can either be trapped by the weight or use it as a life ring and float to the surface. Yet in this very moment, it feels impossible to choose.

I never told her what a difference she made, I thought. *I can't believe she's gone.*

+ + + + + + +

This is an invitation for you.

This is an invitation to stitch moments together in your life, the moments that for some reason lodged between your head and heart. This is an invitation to swim in the complexity and connectedness of your life, to remember the moments, good or bad, that shape who you are today and how you see the world. This is an invitation to dwell in those moments and watch a pattern of who you are today appear. A pattern that has been camouflaged by time, tucked away in the memories and faces of people who have touched your life in some way.

This is an invitation for you.

This is an invitation to stop for a few minutes or a few hours and be curious. Why is it that sometimes these significant moments in our lives show up randomly in the 70,000 reoccurring thoughts we have every day? Do we connect into a collective network that sparks up our memories? Is there an invisible network of moments that have the ability to create hope and inspiration and propel us forward when we need it most? Could it change the world, or has it already? Why do some moments flow through like a swift river and others find a strong hold on our hearts and in our minds?

This is an invitation for you.

This is an invitation to read my story and use it to remember the people in your life that matter. Use it to unlock the infinite power of gratitude, and let it propel you into your own life. Remember what matters or reaffirm what matters. Remember your passion or reaffirm your passion. Remember that we are uniquely connected to each other in a web of moments that is our life.

This is an invitation for you.

This is an invitation to turn gratitude into a verb. Put it in motion and see what happens. Acknowledging people in my life by writing them a letter gave me an opportunity to see myself, not as a series of seemingly disconnected moments, but rather as an integrated pattern of moments that guides who I am today. When I allowed myself to build a bridge between my head and my heart, thinking and feeling, I created an expansive place in my heart for something new.

This is an invitation to see what unfolds for you. Because I really believe we've just touched the surface of what might happen if gratitude became a verb.

THE LETTERS

CHAPTER 3
THE BARISTA &
50 LETTERS

"Hey, Doug! It's my last day! What advice do you have for me?"

"Missy, structure is important in times of change."

"Okay, thanks." I just received a dose of wisdom from a Zen master posing as a barista.

Four days later, I find myself in a coffee shop only two hundred yards from the place my routine used to live. My life is a tornado of thoughts and emotions swirling so fast I can't catch one. I hear a voice and recognize the words: "Missy, structure is important in times of change." Is it the wise barista talking or the voice of God? I decide in that moment to write 50 letters in 50 days to people that made a difference in my life. I just can't go another day feeling this deep regret I have about not reaching out to Ms. Miller.

+ + + + + + +

Sometimes people ask, "Why write a letter? Why not just tell the person?" A participant at a workshop I taught recently answered simply, "Writing a letter creates an intimacy that's hard to achieve with spoken word." She nailed it.

Words on a page are everlasting.

They are a testimony of an experience that can safely reveal details of the heart. Details that in youth seem obvious, but somehow seem dangerous with age.

Abe Lincoln wrote a letter to the Widow Bixby in 1864 to express his gratitude and sympathy for the death of her sons during the civil war. A handwritten letter was his only option. The depth of his feelings can still be felt a century later in the one hundred thirty-seven words he penned. And even though we know him through history books, when we read the words, it is as if his voice and tone live on in the letter.

Sometimes events happen in our own lives that are so big, it's hard to make sense of them, maybe because there is no sense to make. I wonder if this was one of those moments when President Lincoln questioned his faith—questioned if the horrific war was worth all the chaos and death it had created. A war within a nation, where brothers fought brothers and families were divided. An event so big, the magnitude might paralyze even the strongest.

Gratitude provides us with a way to feel a connection to something bigger.

Every one of us wants to know that our life mattered, that there is a reason—a purpose for us being here. I imagine President Lincoln knew this when he expressed his sympathy for the Widow Bixby's loss and yet encouraged her that the death of her sons was not in vain. *"But I cannot refrain from tendering you the consolation that may be found in the thanks of the Republic they died to save."* In these words live a legacy—a written account and reminder that our existence on this earth does matter.

And while the act of writing a letter may seem dated, words on a page have withstood the test of time as a way to convey what we think and how we feel. The page has a way of absorbing the pace of life, and it creates a genuine presence and intimacy lost in other forms of communication. The written word has a way of connecting our head and our heart, exposing something real, something authentic.

Letters have power.

CHAPTER 4
THE FIRST LETTER

I wrote my first letter to my niece, Emma.

I started with her because this rambunctious, spirited little girl holds a special place in my heart. I appreciate the way she sees and feels the world, quietly observing what's happening just below the surface. Do not confuse her quiet disposition as timid, for this young woman is courageous, powerful, and a force to be reckoned with. When she was five or six, her mother and I thought it was time to tell her I was gay. I created a children's book starring her and her brother, Josh. My adult brain thought it would be much easier to discuss the topic of me with a book.

"Emma, I want to talk to you about Aunt Missy," my sister said.

"I know."

"You know what?"

"I know she's gay."

Kids have a sixth sense. They see more than we smart, all-knowing adults would like to believe. Emma's lucky; she still has this sense.

•

There is another reason I chose Emma: she's safe and I had nothing to lose. I've learned along the way that self doubt will show up and beg me not to write a letter because of what might happen. So letter number one had to feel safe. I remember thinking, *Emma might consider me a crazy aunt, but she won't think I'm dumb or silly. I know I can write her a letter, and she will know that there's nothing but love coming from the words on the page. She will just love me.*

Writing Emma a letter gave me a chance to dwell in a moment of gratitude at a time when the world seemed very big. It gave me a chance to reflect on my own freshman year in college. Here's an excerpt from the letter I wrote.

So here's some of the stuff I learned.

1. *I don't test well. Standard test, fill in the blank, etc. I need to experience stuff to learn, THEN, I can beat the pants off of anyone! Sam calls me "primary experience Missy" and it's true.*
2. *Status quo drives me nuts. In fact, I will most likely take a path that hasn't been taken before, over the same path. Rugby? Really? Why not volleyball or some other girl sport?*
3. *Do what you love. In college, I LOVED sports. I had one class in my major, and it's the only class I got a good grade in. Find what you love, and continue to do it. What you love might change. That's ok.*
4. *Don't follow the pack; lead. All my friends went to FSU, so I wanted to go, too. Had I really been listening to myself, I would have gone to a smaller college, possibly gotten a degree in music. Being a leader starts with self, knowing yourself, knowing what matters.*

+ + + + + + +

This letter launched me on a journey through my soul to re-member what really matters by reflecting on the past.

Want to get started? It's simple. Push your noisy mind and all of its excuses out of your way and go.

Here are a few simple letter-writing tips I've learned along the way.

1. *Give without expectation of receiving anything back.*
2. *Listen with your heart.*
3. *Negative gets you negative.*
4. *There is no order in which you should write them.*
5. *Friends are usually easier than family.*
6. *Tell them why you're writing.*
7. *Include a self addressed stamped envelope so they can pay it forward. Ask them to do the same. (It's a revolution.)*
8. *Keep a copy of the letter.*

CHAPTER 5
THE HARDEST LETTER

Day eight.

Dear Mom, I'm not sure what to say.

I try again.

Dear Mom, Thanks for being my mom.
Dear Mom, Why is it easier to write a letter to dad?
Dear Mom, Will you ever sit me on your lap and say, "I am so proud of you and love you so much."? Will it be from a place so deep in your heart that the words will heal the past?

I am searching for something to say to my mom, and it's uncomfortable. I guess it's because a young girl's expectations don't fit in a woman's body. Those feelings belong in the past, and I don't.

The power of this thought seems to crack this chain to the past and frees me from years of waiting for words that may never come.

The gratitude I feel for my mom begins to rise to the surface, and the words follow. It's not a revelation to me that my mom was a person before I was born, but as I write, I begin to imagine my mom as a young girl. These images are created in my mind from stories she has told me, and they piece together a new view, one I haven't seen before.

I picture my mom as a young girl and daughter being raised in the South during the depression. Her mother wears the mask of a homemaker for the family while, under the surface, she is losing the battle to alcohol. I see a young girl sharing a bed with her grandmother, a deeply religious, tobacco-spitting woman. She watches her grandmother regularly curse her own mother as if a daily sermon will exercise the demon alcohol out of her body. I imagine she thinks this is the way life is supposed to be. It is a grown up childhood split between sandcastles on the beach and raising her three brothers.

In her teenage years, evenings usually reserved for a date to the movies are spent with my dad (then her boyfriend) searching for her mom at a local bar and coaxing her home.

The words "love" and "proud" weren't likely to be found in this home for any of these women. Not grandmother, mother, or daughter. This was not a life; it was endurance.

Endurance taught my mother a lot, shaped her—and I believe it shaped me, too.

I'll never forget the day I asked her, "Mom, why did you let an African American girl into your scout troop when you knew it would cause a problem? I remember you telling me that my sister lost her best friend when you did it."

"Well, it was just the right thing to do," she said.

"Just the right thing to do" was a thread that weaved its way throughout her life. In 1961, my dad started a square dance club in Daytona Beach, Florida. There was another square dance club in town, but getting in was by invitation only. Mom thought a club should be open to anyone.

It was just the right thing to do.

Her perseverance and stubbornness are unwavering. She just did it. Naomi Joyce Durant is a poster child for pull yourself up by your bootstraps and keep moving forward. She knew firsthand the importance of being heard, and bootstrapping was the way to get the volume high enough for someone to listen.

At the age of forty-six, she found her own voice. She swapped her June Clever apron for a Gloria Steinem college degree and launched a career in social work. This seemed like a risky move when the normal mid-life choice was either an affair or divorce. I imagine it was just the right thing to do, for her. These are a few moments I dwelled on before I wrote my mom.

+ + + + + + +

After telling this story during a workshop, a participant stopped me and said, "Missy, it's as if you took your mom on your lap and told her, 'I am proud of you. And I love you.'"

Before it was mailed, this letter set me free. Free of expectations never spoken, never realized. Standing at a mailbox, it felt good to mail this letter. A letter with no strings attached. It felt good to let go of years of unfulfilled expectations. This gratitude stuff is hard work. Good work.

Several days later, my phone rang.

"Hi Missy, I got your letter," she said.

"What letter, Mom?"

"It was nice," she said.

That's an interesting response. ("Interesting" is a word I use when I know I am making a judgment. What I really think is, *Seriously? Nice?*)

But instead I ask her, "Well, okay, what'd you think?"

She pauses, "It came out of the blue—and it was hard to absorb. We don't communicate that way."

Is there more? Is that all she's got to say?

"It was easy to read it and let it go by and not think it was important," she says. "I read it, put it aside, then went right back into what I was doing."

"Well, that's good to know."

"I liked it because it made me feel like maybe I had come close to accomplishing my goal of raising you."

"I hope I'm doing a good job with my kids."

"I'm sure you are. Your father and I went to silver sneakers today and the AARP lunch. Anyway, the letter was nice. Thanks."

"Alright, Mom, I'll talk to you later," I say.

"I love you."

This time, I feel her words land on my heart. Three words spoken so many times before that unlock a dam of tears that flood my soul.

I have waited a lifetime to sit on my mother's lap and hear, "Missy, I love you and am so proud of you." Focusing on what I wasn't getting created an emotional booby-trap that is tripped with each conversation. It was a trap that was exposed when I wrote to my mom. It gave me a chance to let the needs of five-year-old Missy go and live in the past where she belongs.

Our stories with our families are connected, woven together by blood and time. We exist both as individuals and a collective, entangled together in the past. It is a past that repeats, sometimes out of habit and sometimes on purpose. Unraveling my life as a daughter with my mother gave me a chance to see us as two people. Two messy human beings living life with all the tools they have.

Viewing my mom's life through my heart of gratitude deepened our relationship and maybe changed a family cycle from endurance to living.

These are the moments I remember now when she says, "I love you."

Grace. Hope. Love. Gratitude. Those things acknowledge humanity...they can exist anywhere...they turn people into valuable stories...they fill people with life...and then they spread. Those things matter because they grab onto human souls and don't let go.

- Dawn Bryant, Pastor, Communicator, and Believer in People

wnat matters

-Grab Your Life-

-Gratitude is a Verb-

CHAPTER 6
GOING NEGATIVE

Everyone should have friends like Julie and Cathy.

Julie is quick-witted, with an unwavering internal strength—an uber-mom who is fiercely loyal to her friends. But most important is her cautiously curious view of the world. Julie asks questions because she is a healthy skeptic.

Cathy is the kind of person you have to lean into hear her voice. This incredible mother never misses a chance for a good quip, is inquisitive, and sees the world through possible eyes. On the eve of day twenty, I got this question, over dinner.

"Are they all positive?" Julie asked me, with her head cocked slightly to one side.

"Of course they are. All of these people have made a difference in my life." *Why would she ask that?*

"Huh." Cathy carefully considers the question and motions for the server.

"I wouldn't read a book just full of positive letters. It's not real." Julie said.

"That's a good point." I pause. "I hadn't considered it from that perspective."

+ + + + + + +

It doesn't take too long to decide. The next morning, I determine letter twenty-one will go to someone I call Mr. Ego. I believe he uses his "power for evil, not good," as a friend of mine used to say. I bet Mr. Ego's friends and family see a different side of him. That's usually the case. My experience was with a person consumed with the dark side of power and money. There is a fine line between good and evil. He crossed that line.

As I park my messenger bag on the couch at the coffee shop, I feel different. For twenty days I have felt light and jiggy when writing a letter. This day is different, as if the memories of working with this man are waking up from a long nap. I take a deep breath and begin the letter like I did every other, telling him why I am writing letters to people in my life.

This feels phony. I don't really care if he knows why. He won't give a shit anyway, I think.

I am committed, so I continue writing, and dark, painful feelings begin to take shape and form into letters on the page. The words flow quickly as I relive the memories and experiences I encountered over a year's time. The words flow so quickly that time stands still. My body fills with anger, frustration, and disgust as I am writing. The negative energy continues to grow and spread through my body as my fingers strike the keyboard.

Dear Sir,
Here's what I learned from you:
I learned that at all cost, doing something at all cost, really has a

cost. I want to believe you began with good intent as I watched you time and time again use negative reinforcement or someone's failure to motivate them. That has a cost, and it wasn't pretty. I learned that it takes both, a male perspective and a female perspective, to run a business. The tactics you used were like driving a group of Navy Seals. Appropriate for Navy Seals.

I learned that your words and behaviors were not aligned. I agree with many of your philosophies about leadership, and that teaching great leaders to lead is important. I believe you have a very different definition of leader than I do. Your definition seemed to be confined to title and hierarchy. I think the point you missed was that focusing on just the top might get you a gig, but it does not create a cultural shift. You missed the point that it takes both, leadership from the grassroots AND leadership from the top.

I learned that you have conditional respect. When I was trying to put together a meeting, I flew out to meet you in Baltimore to try to talk about what we might do. I waited around late into the evening, and when we finally did "talk," it was as if you just checked the box, patted me on the head, and moved me along—so you could say to a person in power, you did it. Respect is not conditional. Real respect requires listening.

I have two children, and I would not want them to randomly survey people I work with and find out that human shrapnel is my human capital strategy.

So, in the end, you did make a difference in my life. You reinforced what I don't want to be.

Take THAT! I think, or maybe even say out loud as I slam my laptop closed. I feel myself swimming in queasiness, and disgust.

+ + + + + + +

Greed, power, money.

These were only story lines in books, on screen and in fairy tales, until I met this man and realized there are people in the world actually motivated by these words. So consumed and driven by power and greed, he seemed to have become blind, aloof, and detached from the impact of his behavior on people around him. He paid homage to those with positional power and created an illusion of raising voices not heard.

Each relationship had, not value, but a *value to him*. If it benefited him, it was sacred. If it didn't, it was shrapnel. He walked on the very values I believe are important. To me he was a force of darkness in the world, motivated by power and his ego fed by greed.

Writing this letter, I discovered energy is unbiased. It finds momentum and flows.

The negative emotions I felt were useful in the moment, propelling me forward to write the letter. In the darkness of the negative emotions, I learned that without darkness, there would be no light. Without negative, there would be no positive.

The Persian poet and philosopher Rumi said, "God turns you from one feeling to another and teaches by means of opposites so you will have two wings to fly, not one."

Hours after I finished the letter, toxicity lingered in my body. I knew if I ignored these emotions they would curl up in a tight ball somewhere in my body and wait. This letter was another lesson in letting go and taking back power unintentionally given away.

It's like the story a friend once told me of a great army general during a civil war in Japan, pushing through the hillsides, leaving destruction in his path. He came upon a temple where a monk sat quietly meditating, and this angered the general, accustomed as he was to fear. He stood in front of the motionless monk and yelled, "Don't you understand I can run my sword through your heart?!"

Quietly the monk looked up and replied, "Don't you understand I am a man with a choice?"

+ + + + + +

It took me purposeful, focused attention to reverse the negative spiral. This experience grounded my respect for using power for good, not evil. It cemented my belief in people being heard, regardless of hierarchy and positional power.

Getting to the heart of why this was such a negative experience for me created a choice. I don't have the same negative feelings when I think of this man now. I took back the power I had given away. When I let go of the negative feelings, it opened up a different view for me to see and feel grateful for the lessons I learned.

I never sent the letter. I didn't need to.

Before you write a negative letter, ask yourself:
+ Is there a negative experience that comes to mind?
+ Does this experience play a recurring role in your life or memories?
+ What has been your experience with this person?
+ When you recall the memories or moments, what emotions do you feel?

After you write the letter, ask yourself:
+ How do you feel now?
+ When the recipient opens and reads the letter, will it surprise him/her? Will it change this person's behavior? Could it potentially have the same negative impact on the recipient's life as he/she has had on yours?
+ Step back and look at the experience from a distance. Is there

anything you've learned that you can use from this point on?
+ Is it possible you've been holding onto something that's not useful to you anymore?

Notice how negative attracts negative. You can choose to move through the negative – notice it, acknowledge it, and move past it. Remember to be gentle with yourself. Many times growth is like circles continuously overlapping and moving forward.

Rarely is there a "there" at any point in your journey—only markers along the way.

CHAPTER 7
LETTER TO THE DEAD

It's the winter of 1988, and for as long as I can remember, the battle with my mom has been an undercurrent that changes speeds unpredictably. She believes I dropped out of college for a job. The truth is I dropped out of college to make money and get far away from my small hometown. But I've let my mom believe that my life is so exciting, I rarely have time for anything else.

"Your Uncle Tom is very sick." I have taken this call a few times before in the last few years. My uncle has been sick a lot.

"Ok." I swing my feet to the ground, ready to end the call.

"You really should drive over to see him. He's in a coma, Missy."

"Mom, I'm really busy here. I'm the manager on duty."

Silence follows. It is the kind of silence woven into the DNA of every mother to use as their last line of defense. "Okay."

Now I am in my car, driving towards Daytona Beach to see a man in a coma.

+ + + + + + +

I stand outside the hospital room next to my mom as she prepares me for what I am about to see.

"Just talk to him like he is awake."

Well, that's a problem, I think, *since most of our conversations are usually very short.*

I take a deep breath, summoning courage and a smile, and follow my mom into the room. It's white. Everything is white, except for the silver. White and silver. I wonder if hospitals intentionally use these colors saved for heaven.

Uncle Tom is laying in bed at a 30 degree angle, eyes staring across the room, seemingly fixed on the blank white wall at the foot of his bed.

I walk over to the left side of his bed and slowly reach over the silver bar to touch his hand. It is warm, like the warmth of his heart. The warmth I always felt but we never talked about. "Hi Tom, it's Missy." It sounds stupid. I search for something profound to say, something interesting about my life—the life of a middle manager. There are no words. I hate my job.

And so I just stand here in all of my discomfort and hold his hand for what seems like hours.

But then something happens.

Uncle Tom's eyes brighten. The room fills with life, replacing the lingering threat of death that was here when I walked in. He looks at me, holds my eyes with his.

"Missy, life is too short to do the things you don't want to do."

A message.

Then, as quickly as the room filled with life, it empties. Stunned, I walk out of the room, my mom following closely behind.

"What just happened in there?" I hear my mom say as if from a distance, even though she is right behind me. "His eyes changed."

I stand for a moment, steadying myself, so off balance that the weight of my eyes blinking quickly might be enough to tip me over.

"What...just...happened?" she says again. If anyone is going to see the image of Jesus on a shower curtain, it will be my mother. This is a moment made for her, not me. I don't believe in all that stuff.

"He got a message to me..." I lean against the wall.

"His lips didn't move, Missy."

"I know." I feel the enormity of the moment, the busyness of the hall, and the need for my feet to run fast. But I stand still and let it wash over me.

+ + + + + + +

Two days later, there is no coma, only death. Two days later, the weight of the message sinks in. Life presented me a billboard hard to ignore. Two months later, I use my 401k to go back to college for the fifth time. This time, I do it because I want to, and I study something I love.

I imagine Uncle Tom smiling.

+ + + + + + +

Day thirty-three I wrote a letter to a dead man. It was a short letter, like most of our conversations. I filled him in on the mundane facts of my life since his death. I told him about my degrees, both of them. I told him about finding love, starting a family, and moving out of the South. I reminded him that he was the impetus to my seemly risky behavior of following my passion. Because of what happened, I had taken risks piled on top of risks in my life that started in a hospital room that was filled with life and death. I told him I missed him but, somehow, I knew he was still with me.

I wish I would have known Tom as an adult.

He was an ordinary guy. The youngest of four kids, he spent his time in the Navy as a cook and loved comic books. After the Navy, he held down several different jobs as a cook for a while and spent most of his time alone. I will never know what happened in his life to make him want to leave early. I guess he was just done being here. He tried to commit suicide several times. His body finally surrendered in 1988.

Writing a letter to Uncle Tom gave me a chance to reflect on his life, the moments before his death, and the impact he has had on my life ever since. His life mattered. I don't think he felt that way, but I do.

Gratitude isn't saved for the living. It's available whenever you are, reaching the past, the future, or today.

I wrote a letter to a dead guy and sent it to heaven on the wings of a flame.

-notes-

"Feeling the love and safety of other's positive energy unleashes your own potential and the potential of so many others."

- Julie Gilbert, CEO/Founder Wolf Means Business

-Gratitude is a Verb-

-Grab Your Life-

CHAPTER 8
THE BIGGEST RISK OF ALL

Day fifty, and I am excited and scared. This completes my commitment. I've been saving this day for someone really special. I sit down and stare at the page. No words appear. I feel pressure to get this one right, because the stakes are high. I stare and, instead of words, I remember the day more than a decade ago when I opened my heart again like I was sixteen.

+ + + + + +

I can do this. Self pep talk is a recurring theme in my life. I pace the small apartment and say it out loud. "What's the worst that can happen? She'll think I'm crazy? She'll smile and say, 'That's nice?' Oh, god, what am I doing?" I stop. "I can do this."

As I answer myself, there is a knock at the door. The seconds it takes to walk to the door seem to disappear. My hand freezes on the handle for a moment. I take in as much air as I can to fuel my courage and open the door.

"Hi!" Her voice is filled with an optimistic melody that makes the single-syllable word vibrate the whole room.

"Hi, Sam!" *Well, that sounded stupid. But what else can I say? I could have said….* I stop the conversation in my head before she hears it. "Come on in. The other girls from work aren't here yet. Can I get you something to drink? A Cosmo?"

Lord knows I need one. I walk to the kitchen without waiting for an answer, and she's following me, saying something, but I can't hear the words over the voice in my head.

Just tell her.

I remember the evening I first saw her, seven years before. She walked into the room of a fundraiser I was attending. I did a double take, partly because of her striking beauty, but mostly because I had a strange sense that I had known her before. It was as if every cell in my body was waking up from a slumber. I didn't understand it then, but I do now.

And now I'm feeling those same emotions all over again. In the kitchen, I begin busying myself mixing a drink, making small talk while fighting with my internal voice.

Ok—now! What are you waiting for? Just do it. Don't miss your chance!

As I hand her a drink, I see her again for the first time. Her smiling blue eyes and short black hair take my breath away. The warmth of her smile calms me for a moment.

"Cheers!" she says brightly.

"Cheers," I reply, catching her eye. "Samantha, I have something to tell you." I take another big gulp and hope liquid courage isn't a myth.

"What is it?" she asks, with a sweet, unsuspecting smile.

We are walking towards the living room.

I...I am in love with you. There, I said it.

Wait, no, I didn't. My lips didn't move.

She sits on the sofa, looks at me, and smiles again. "What is it, Missy?"

"I'm in love with you." The words I rehearsed spill out of my mouth so fast it sounds like one word. The look on her face changes from smile to surprise. *Is it surprise?*

I hear a knock at the door.

Oh crap. The girls are here. We need to leave for the party. I just spilled my guts. Did she hear what I said? I have no idea what she thinks. *Crap!* I take another big sip and answer the door, afraid to make eye contact with her. Just in case it was only surprise.

+ + + + + + +

Four hours later driving home from the party, I consider my options. *Don't make eye contact, open the door, wave goodnight, and pretend none of this ever happened. No harm, no foul, we keep our friendship. I am sure she's forgotten what I said.*

Excellent plan. As she pulls into the driveway, I make eye contact and my entire plan unravels.

She touches my face softly with her hand and kisses me goodnight.

+ + + + + + +

And that kiss begins a life filled with love. A life so big, it must be a dream or a book. Because only in a dream would there be a perfect fit like this. Only in a book would two people share a mind and soul.

That's the only explanation for the last eleven years—I am living a dream.

She is my soul mate. I know, soul mate sounds so eye-rollingly New Agey, but I can't find another explanation for what we have.

I close my eyes and remember moments, trivial and full, weaving a tapestry of love, moments when for no reason and every reason our hearts have touched and we've shared a breath.

Planting flowers in the front yard. Sitting by the river watching the sunset. Buying our first house. Reading the Sunday paper at the diner. Feeling her belly and knowing it's a girl. Pushing a stroller around the lake while that baby girl finally sleeps. Walking around the block on September 7, 2005, counting minutes between contractions. Holding that little boy after he's born. The curtains blowing into the apartment in Italy during a nap. Lying on a beach in Hope Town. Listening to our song.

Three pages later, I realize I am sobbing, so overwhelmed with how lucky I am. I know love—something I never thought was possible when I walled off my heart that day sitting on the edge of a yellow flowered bedspread.

I fold the last letter and, this time, I decide to deliver the letter. I want Sam to know now that all the moments have mattered.

It's just the right thing to do.

If the letter you want to write feels so big there are no words, close your eyes and settle into all of the small moments. You may find pages of gratitude await you.

-notes-

"What matters...how we live our lives, how we treat others, creating as many possible special memories with family and friends."

- Ginger Harris, Community Organizer, Business Professional, Friend

what matters
-Grab Your Life-

-Gratitude is a Verb-

THE PROCESS

CHAPTER 9
CIRCLES & PATTERNS

Mary knows me well, which in this case is quite irritating. I am a functional introvert. I like back seats. Meeting new people is a painful and awkward event.

When I walk in the door, I notice there is no back to this group. It is a circle. Circles have meaning.

And I am screwed.

"Hi!" It's Mary.

"I can't believe you didn't tell me about this," I said through clenched teeth.

"If I would have told you, you wouldn't have come," Mary says with a mischievous twinkle in her eyes. She quickly introduces me to the nice women behind the obligatory draped folding table sealing my fate.

Then I hear a bell. Bells have meaning. As the bell is struck in a slow meaning-filled rhythm, I roll my eyes and shake my head, reminded that not participating is not an option.

There is one way into the circle, and I follow Mary. I practically sit on top of her, I'm so nervous. I'm sure it is a beautiful room, because I know we are in an art gallery, but I have no time to notice beauty; I am still plotting my escape. How do I escape a circle with one opening? If I run through the middle, I'll knock over the flowers in the center.

Someone begins to speak, and the only part I catch is "...and we'll each take a turn, passing this ball and introducing ourselves."

Shit. I hate this. Why am I here? A layer of sweat covers my body. I watch the ball move around the circle. People are introducing themselves and saying something clever.

Shit. Shit. Shit. I look down, and the ball is in my hands.

"Missy," is all I say. I force the ball into Mary's hands.

She looks at me.

The last person with the ball is the author, and he begins to speak with a slow, deliberate cadence. He is a great storyteller. I know this technique well, because it's in my arsenal. He is talking about a trip to Africa. It's a story that represents meaning for him. He's done this before. Half listening and trying to see my watch, I feel his cadence change. "Now, move into smaller circles, with no more than four people...."

What did he just say?! "Now, move into smaller circles, with no more than four people..."

Nooooooooo! My thought is so loud that my body jerks, and I look around. No one has heard me.

"...and answer the question, 'What matters?'"

As if drawn together like magnets, chairs and people began to form circles. I attach myself to Mary. We form a circle with two other women whom I'm pretty sure crossed the mid-life line before me.

Breathe. Breeeaaathe. I can do this. No, I can't. Yes, I can.

I bet everyone can see the sweat forming on my face.

I feel the room shrinking as my vision narrows. Fainting is one way to escape a circle, but I'm not that lucky today. It's the fifty-three muscles in my face contracting at the same time.

Breathe in, breathe out —I can hear my yoga instructor's voice in my head, and it's enough to help my face begin to relax. Or maybe my knees touching strange knees brings me back to the moment. The owners of the knees each take a turn, answering the question. I don't really hear the answers, but I can tell that they hit the mark. The circle nods in unison like a shelf of bobble heads.

Perfect. They all have an answer. Can they hear my thoughts? God, I hope not.

They are looking at me, and I realize it's my turn to answer the question. I am not ready, because I've been holding my breath... or maybe the oxygen found a way out of the circle. Lucky oxygen. I imagine the earth stops spinning and tilts on its axis to listen.

"What matters?" I say. Motionless, I look into strangers' eyes. "I don't know. I'm trying to figure it out."

The earth didn't stop, there is oxygen in the room, and the wise women bobble their heads and smile. Life has a funny way of showing up just when I need it and, sometimes, even when I think I don't.

+ + + + + + +

Moments present themselves often. We get to choose when to listen with our soul.

Running life at break-neck speed is the badge of an overachiever. Standing at the crossroads of my life, the question, "What matters?" seemed daunting. I knew that I should have the answer. I got paid to know. Not knowing is like waving the white flag of defeat and career suicide.

I'm not sure what came over me in the circle when I admitted I didn't know the answer. I just said it. In that moment, it felt like I was floating in the world seeing through the eyes of a child again, assumption and burden free.

A few seconds beyond this breakthrough moment, I was terrified again. Old habits are hard to break.

Knowing is a habit.

The path in front of me is paved with not knowing. I once saw a gas station sign that said, "Wisdom knows you don't know." Bad grammar, good point.

Every letter I wrote had personal meaning. It wasn't until I was halfway through writing 50 letters that I noticed the pattern of what was really important to me. Hidden in the pattern like a *Where's Waldo* was my answer to the "What matters?" question. It wasn't a new answer or an epiphany. It was simply there all along, waiting for me to notice.

+ + + + + + +

I use a simple pattern when I write letters. First, I open with a short sentence or two describing what I am doing. Next I tell them why they made an impact on my life. Finally, I always close with a thank you.

The heart in each letter is step two – the specific why.

Here are a couple examples of how I think about being specific. If I have a memory of a moment that had a lasting impact on my life, I retell the story from my point of view.

On day six, I wrote a letter to my Uncle Dick. Some people simply see my uncle as a high school math teacher and track coach. I see him as a farmer, planting seeds of knowledge through self-discovery. He planted seeds through the experience of learning, then watered the seeds by making everything available for his students and athletes to be successful. The rest of the growth was up to them. I imagine life is a mathematical equation for my uncle. Passion plus experience and practice equals success. He gave every student the chance to learn and cultivated those students and athletes with real passion.

He saw a passion for running in me at the age of nine, planted a seed and watched it grow. I will never forget the look on his face, when I showed him the gold medal I won in the 1998 Amsterdam Gay Games. It was the look of pride and joy from a life's work that matters.

Here's an excerpt from the letter I sent to my Uncle Dick:

February 22, 2009
Dear Uncle Dick,

I was packing up my office…when I found a mug that you gave me a long time ago. I don't know if you remember it or not. It says "Those who can, teach. Those who can't go into some less significant line of work." I remember looking at it and laughing that of all the stuff I have shuffled around from place to place, this mug has been a constant. And it made me think about you.

I think I carried it from place to place because I believe that teaching is a gift. It's the ability to combine information with experience and a bit of wisdom that invites someone to learn. You have done that with me for as long as I can remember. I can close my eyes and remember standing on the track in Daytona Beach at a city meet, and you teaching me the proper running technique for my arms. I bet I was about nine. Then, you entered me in every event at the meet! And I mean every event—from shot put, to high jump, to the 100-yard dash. I'm guessing it was either part of your master plan to try stuff out, or you told my mom you'd take me for the day, and it kept me busy either way.

I learned two things. First, I started to figure out what I liked and didn't like. Shot put, high jump—out. 100 yard dash—out. Longer stuff—ok. Second, all of the running stuff gave me a chance to work on technique over and over again. You would give me a few tips in between and words of encouragement. You were giving me a chance to learn by doing. And when you teach that way, it sticks. To this day, when I am running and am getting tired, I still think about that coaching, and I adjust my arms and stride.

+ + + + + + +

When I wrote this letter, I slipped back in time to the moment when we were standing on the track. Viewing the scene as if it were a private showing of a movie I'd held onto for years, I started writing. I knew it was a story from my heart because I could feel the day again. I remembered being nine, the temperature that day, how big the track looked, and being scary-excited that I would be on my own all day.

If I could feel the moment again, it meant it was coming from my heart.

But sometimes when I write a letter, it isn't one moment, but years of moments that have made an impact on my life. Mr. Courson was my high school band teacher. He had a strict disciplinary style in which every choice and behavior had a consequence, and I imagine students and parents sometimes confused his style with not caring, although that couldn't have been farther from the truth. This was a man who cared very much.

Our school football team got the field for practice, which meant that our band practice got to take place in a parking lot full of cars, but Mr. Courson believed we deserved a field, too. So he made a deal with a business nearby that had a large lot behind their building. Every August he'd mow the field and line it with hash marks, so we could rehearse. During rehearsal, he'd park his blue Scout on the fifty-yard line, hop out in his plaid Bermuda shorts, and climb onto the hood with his bullhorn. We'd march up and down the field until the new freshmen could hold a straight line between the hash-marks, and only then would he unroll pages of large graph paper on the hood of the Scout and unveil the show, which he choreographed from scratch every year.

Mowing a large field with a small mower every year in the heat of the summer in Florida is the act of someone with deep respect for both his profession and the young band geeks he helps shape.

Mr. Courson also had high expectations. Year after year, his bands were at the top of any competition he entered. His leadership style was heavy on practice and discipline, because that was the way he helped us reach those high expectations. He taught us respect through his actions.

Here's an excerpt from the letter I wrote to Mr. Courson:

I also learned discipline—and that doing the right thing wasn't always the popular thing. I remember when some of my friends left skid marks on the field we practiced on. And I remember having to make a decision to do the right thing, or do the popular thing. I remember at the time what a tough decision that was, when I had to come to you and tell you and then had to discipline my friends. I remember you were mad.... and you supported me. Not with your words, but with the look you had on your face. The look of, I know this will be hard, but it will be ok.

That is a leadership lesson that has shaped how I make tough decisions every day. When I was responsible for human resources for all the Best Buy stores in the U.S., and some of the leaders had made bad decisions—and these were well-respected leaders—we let some of them go. It wasn't the popular decision, but it was the right decision. I guess Best Buy ought to thank you, too!

I also learned about "conducting" a group of people. Whether band or orchestra, there is something amazing about a group of individuals finding a way to come together, everyone doing their part, to make something bigger. It's part of who I am today and what I believe and do. I try to see the potential in every person and help them find a way to fit into something bigger. Whether it's a short note on a triangle or a French horn solo, both are unique and important, and the world needs them. Finding the right timing is all that is needed.

+ + + + + + +

Mr. Courson made a difference in my life and the lives of others. He demanded respect, because he led with respect. He demanded high expectations because he led with high expectations. Mr. Joseph Courson passed away on January 11, 2008, at the age of 80. I wrote him a letter a year later, not knowing he was gone. An old high school friend helped me locate his daughter, and I sent the letter to her. I wanted her to know the Joe I knew.

Both of these men were passionate about their professions. In both of these men, their words and behaviors aligned. Behaviors like learning, discipline, and practice. These are three of the behaviors I found reoccurring in the letters I wrote. I learned that the answer to the question, "What matters?" was both in my own behaviors and in the behaviors of those people that have had an impact on my life.

The heart of the letter is in the why.

+ + + + + + +

When you sit down to write:
+ Be still.
+ Be specific.
+ Trust yourself.

Trust yourself. When you write a letter from the heart, it carries a message that is believable. It pumps life into your letter. It creates a place for memories, usually reserved for your own recall, to flow. It leaves a record and legacy of the impact someone made on the world, and a glimpse at what's important to you. The heart of your letter is in the why.

-notes-

"What Matters... is the ability to 'mine' your life experiences – ups and downs - to lead with courage and compassion"

- Kal Patel, Vantagepoint Capital Partners

-Gratitude is a Verb-

wnat matters
-Grab Your Life-

CHAPTER 10
THRESHOLDS

I was a Girl Scout. I suppose I still am.

I started as a Brownie in elementary school and ended my Girl Scout experience as a Junior. Being a Junior is a very big deal. It meant making my way through days and years, through badges and mint cookies in green boxes stacked high in my parents' garage, through campfires, s'mores and scary ghost stories. It meant riding my bike to the church community room a mile away, once a week and crossing a very busy street with a stoplight to get there. It meant remembering to wear my uniform on meeting days, tucking my Girl Scout Manual into the basket of my bike, and doing my best on the current project I was working on for a badge. Becoming a Junior was a very big deal.

I remember the day I "flew up" to Junior. I remember it like it was yesterday.

+ + + + + +

Here we are, Troop 448, standing in our green jumpers, white pinfold shirts, green knee socks, green beret, and a sash filled with badges sewed on by hand. Badges that taught us important skills like sewing, making a fire, safety, and helping someone across the street. The badges were how we were measured—how our scout leader knew we were ready. Ready for the next step on our Girl Scout journey. It would take me years to learn that sometimes lessons are less in the actual doing of one activity, but in all the activities combined.

Badges are important, but it's the sash that holds it all together.

The blue sky is peeking from behind the clouds; Mother Nature is winking at us. We, the Brownies in Troop 448, stand on one side of a wooden bridge that crosses a small man-made stream in the Ormond Beach Memorial Museum and Gardens. On the other side stand the women scout leaders in their green uniforms, standing tall, looking proud and serious, likely remembering a day of passage of their own. This is a ritual that thousands of girls have experienced before us.

As our troop leaders start to announce names, I feel myself getting nervous. It is alphabetical order, so I know they will call my name soon. I watch friends take turns walking over the bridge.

"Missy Durant." My scout leader uses a staccato voice.

Hearing my name surprises me and I jump.

Everyone's looking at me. *Don't trip. Hurry up and get across,* I think. I hurry across the bridge.

That was easy—and awkward. Glad that's done.

There is a swirl of seemingly unconnected thoughts pooling in my head. *Now what do I do? Stand still? Hard to stand still. Adjust my skirt? I hate wearing skirts. What if I want to climb a tree? Just wait. Oh, here comes Sandy. I wonder if the water's cold? Wow, I'm a Junior.*

I don't feel any different. I hope we get cupcakes. Chocolate. Red punch. Yeah! Wait, she's still talking.

+ + + + + +

As quickly as it started, it was over. I remember thinking I didn't feel any different. I didn't feel smarter or suddenly have the ability to sell more Girl Scout cookies. But something was different. I was a Junior, and I knew in my head that was different, because I walked over a bridge and was handed wings. I had entered the door to Junior-dom. I was supposed to be different now; I just didn't know what that meant. And the beauty of being a young girl was that it was ok to not know.

I remembered this moment again when I was writing letters. Because moments are all we have, and together they weave a story of who we are. Moments are like laughter—a universal force, not bound by the color of our skin, the language we speak, or the century we live in. Moments contain stories from our past worth examining and honoring. We can stand in these moments and let them flow through us, to live again or let it go.

In this memory, I discover a threshold.

Thresholds are the in-between and an entryway for change, an opportunity, and chance to learn. A doorway to stand in, look through, walk through, and when you are ready—or not—emerge on the other side, breathing new air in a new moment.

Thresholds have been a symbol for transition for thousands of years. Grooms carry their brides across a threshold to symbolize a new beginning. John the Baptist immersed people in water to symbolize washing away their past and beginning something new. Celebrating an eighteenth birthday in the United States gives us the right to vote. Walk across a stage accompanied by pre-recorded version of pomp and circumstance, grab your diploma, and walk into adulthood.

We are surrounded by thresholds.

But I believe there is another kind of threshold. These are the thresholds that are without ritual or clarity. We walk through these, and it's only when we look back that we realize they were an important moment in our life. Like sitting in a yellow room, or standing in a hospital room, or crossing a bridge. These are thresholds in hindsight. Doors we walk through and then find ourselves on the other side of our lives.

Every one of us has a threshold story. A story that gives us an opportunity to rejoin the cast in that moment. When we give ourselves the chance to shine a light on that moment, we remember that life in an instant has meaning. Thresholds provide us with a choice, a doorway that when we walk through it, gives us the ability to take inventory and discard things we might not need anymore. When we find ways to leave behind the thoughts and behaviors we no longer need, it opens up room for something else.

Thresholds are powerful.

CHAPTER 11

GRATITUDE IS A VERB

Sentences need verbs the way life needs movement.

A verb is a part of speech that expresses existence or action, and without verbs, sentences are just fragments. Without action, our gratitude is a fragment of what it could be.

Research by Martin Seligman, the founder of positive psychology, revealed that people who write "gratitude letters" to someone who made a difference in their lives score higher on happiness and lower on depression—and the effect lasts for weeks.

I believe it's because gratitude is a verb.

A verb demands action, movement, progress. A verb expects that each of us take a step and move from the world of good intent into a world of action. Not just action for action's sake, but the action of *being* a human being...doing. A human being doing things for others. What would happen if each one of us set the word gratitude in motion, turned the focus from ourselves, and unleashed it back into the world? Maybe—just maybe—gratitude is a gift, just like children are a gift. A gift for us to hold for a time, then release again for the world to own.

Time is a precious commodity for me.

I have arrived at midlife, and I can tell you it's not a crisis at all, but a gift. I choose to regain my identity, to reclaim the parts of me that I had buried for a while, to reinvent the person I am today. The time I've spent writing letters has contained an intense amount of reflection and been a stark reminder of the way our lives are held together by moments.

Life is full of moments. Some are big "M" moments, and some are little "m" moments. There have been so many people in my life that have made an impact in some way. There are those I remember and wrote a letter to, and there are still thousands more.

Somewhere along the way I started breathing again. Because it was so simple, the act of gratitude in motion. This book is an honoring of those moments that have lodged in between my head and my heart.

My stories and words are meant as a gift to you. Words and stories that nudge you to look in that small space—the twelve inches between your head and your heart—and remember and feel the moments in your life that matter. In that small space is a powerful energy source called gratitude.

This is an invitation.

An invitation to create *your* own practice and gratitude revolution, because gratitude really is a verb.

THE PRACTICE

CHAPTER 12
PRACTICE #1—LISTEN

As a functional introvert, listening is not just a skill, it's a strategy used to limit the number of times I experience that horrible, awkward feeling of not knowing what to say next to the person I hardly know.

A well-skilled listener uses their craft to listen not just to words, but for the meaning behind the words—the feelings in the words—and the real story behind the story. It is a skill available to everyone, and yet practiced by few.

Jen is a well-skilled listener.

Jen and I have logged hundreds of miles running and have finished two marathons together. In the rhythmic pounding of miles and hours, Jen and I talk about the most mundane topics, from politics to our favorite place to get a hamburger. We have shared our happiest stories from childhood and our deepest fears in life. Running is meditative for both of us. Running is the vehicle for our deep friendship, and running a marathon was a marker in time.

+ + + + + + +

November 4, 2004, at The New York City Marathon: Jen and I crowd with thirty thousand other runners at the start to run the 26.2 miles through the burrows of New York City. It is a beautiful day, and running through the first few burrows is magical. The streets are lined with spectators cheering, handing out hard candy, hands reaching out for a good luck high-five. The faces, young and old, that line the streets, change with each burrow. Complete silence falls upon us as we descend into the Jewish Hassidic neighborhood. The only sound is 60,000 running-shoe-clad feet hitting the ground.

It is magical, and from the start, the energy is radiating.

That energy and excitement carries me to mile 21 when, like so many marathoners before me, I hit the wall. It's the point when the race becomes less about physical ability and more about mental endurance. My back, my neck, my hip, my knees ache...and it's hot. Too hot for girls who trained in the snow days before. I pause at the water stop and pour water on my head to cool down. It doesn't work. I'm falling prey to the mile 21 demons.

"My back is killing me," I pant. Leaning over attempting to stretch only makes it worse.

"Keep walking through the water stop. We'll run when we get to the last table," Jen says.

But I know that when I get to that table I am not running another step. I had decided. I keep walking and Jen follows.

"You go ahead. I'll meet you at the finish."

"We trained together, we finish together," she says. Jen grabs my hand with a determination so grounded in belief it moves us both forward. Slowly we run again.

+ + + + + + +

Jen knew me, she listened to my stories, and she knew that this was something I could do, with a little support. Jen knew because she listens. She hears the story, the words, and the space between those words. She knew I had 5.2 miles left in me and that the pain in my back was more mental than physical. As we crossed the finish line together, I remember that feeling—a sense of accomplishment and a raw, deep gratitude for a friend whose gift to the world is listening.

The race itself was amazing, and those 26.2 miles will remain on my list of highlights. But the race was nothing compared to all those miles Jen and I ran together beforehand and the deep sense of gratitude I feel whenever I think of Jen.

Theoretically, listening is simple. So is cooking. On a recent trip to Italy, I was reminded of how few ingredients Italians use to cook a meal: seasonal ingredients, a drizzle of olive oil, some sea salt, and a dash of fresh basil or rosemary. I love Italy. After each meal, I would announce to the table that when I got back to my kitchen, I would cook just like this!

Three weeks later, I confidently made a trip to the grocery store to get my ingredients to cook a fine Italian meal for my family. Much to my surprise, even though I used the same simple ingredients, my meal tasted nothing like the meal I had at Da Pietro in Rome.

Sometimes simple is anything *but* simple.

Millions of dollars have been spent on communication training, each with lists of five to ten steps to better listening. Usually the lists consist of some combination of being attentive, avoiding formulating a response before the person is finished talking, asking clarifying questions, and watching for body language cues. Simple in theory and yet, just like cooking, add a human being or two to the equation and complexity follows.

Listening is foundational to living a life of gratitude. It's important because it is rare. And it's rare because it is hard. It's hard because we are adults. Because for most of us, being an adult means knowing. When we enter a conversation knowing, we miss the beauty of the moment to listen and learn.

Begin your listening practice with yourself.

There lives a list in your head of people that have made an impact on your life. It lives in your head, surrounded by good intent. One minute is the amount of time it takes to calm the mind enough and slow down the approximately 70,000 thoughts we have each day. Sixty seconds to cull through those thoughts and turn good intent into action.

Sit quietly right where you are. Take a deep breath and when you are ready, close your eyes. Notice your chest and shoulders rise with each breath in, and how they fall with each breath out.

Ask yourself these questions:
+ Who am I grateful for?
+ Who has made an impact on my life?
+ Who has mattered?

Listen and notice who comes to mind. Take another deep breath. Let your eyes open when they are ready. By reigniting memories of the people that impacted your life, you experience the first wave of gratitude. Dwell in the gratitude for a moment, and write the names of those who came to mind in no particular order.

Imagine a still lake. Imagine picking up a rock, and throwing it into the lake. Notice the circle in the center; at the core it is smaller, more concentrated. As the circles move farther from the center, they become larger, less defined, and yet still a connected part of the core circle in the center.

People in our lives are like a drop of water in a pond.

There are a smaller number of friends and family who are core to our lives, and farther from the core are people that are in or have touched our lives along the way, like friends, colleagues, and teachers. These are people that have made a difference in your life.

Seeing the names on the list can create dueling emotions, igniting the intense and overwhelming feeling of gratitude and an emotional fear that's triggered by the thought of sharing what feels like intimate thoughts on paper.

You decide.

You may like to ease into this process by choosing someone less emotionally threatening, or dive into the center of your life and write someone very close to your heart.

The important part is you decide.

As you practice, you will build muscle, courage, and strength to write letters to those closest to you.

Begin your practice today and trust yourself.

-notes-

"What Matters...The moment we realize there is something deeper then the popular pursuits of existence, mixed with the courage to find the things that give us life."

\- Daniel Gutierrez, Pastor, Blogger, Husband, Dad

-Gratitude is a Verb-

CHAPTER 13
PRACTICE #2
BE WHERE YOU ARE

I wonder if my parents felt big and grown up when they attended my school performances in elementary school forty years ago. Because I sure do.

The gym is filled with rows of cheap folding chairs all facing a stage with standard issue, long, green, velvet curtains in need of cleaning.

"Is this seat taken?" I ask.

There is no response from the man in the chair next to the empty one. He shakes his head back and forth without taking his eyes off his Blackberry.

I sit down.

Man, I've been that guy. I am flooded with gratitude and empathy. I've been that guy. Working even when I wasn't. I turn and focus on the stage as the first graders start to fill the risers.

Angels. It's the only possible explanation for why they don't fall off the risers. I return the smiles and waves of kids searching the crowded gym for their people. My daughter finds me and gives me a little wave-smile.

I glance at the guy next to me again, still tapping the Blackberry. *Look up!* I think hard, hoping he can hear me.

He doesn't.

The gym fills with energy as the first graders start to sing. Everyone there is proud of someone. The kids sing, smile, and wave.

He doesn't look up.

They twist, straighten, and twitch.

His oversized fingers tap on the phone.

They yawn, tap, yell, dance, and clap for twenty minutes, followed by a bow that looks more like the wave. It is rewarded with thunderous applause.

He looks up for a moment, stands, and walks away.

+ + + + + + +

This is a true and sad story. Not for the obvious reasons that he wasn't fully present and attentive for his child's performance, but for the less obvious one. The one that is a picture of the constant pursuit of more and the never ending search for happiness we find ourselves racing toward.

This could be a modern day Norman Rockwell painting. A parent's unending attachment, dedication, and attention to work and the appointment they had to attend.

We are working harder and longer as a society than we ever have, and we aren't any happier.

Time is precious.

It feels like a stinging statement meant to somehow shock us into a new behavior, where we instantly transform, wake up, and realize the error of our way. Instead blanket statements like this seem to drive us to work harder to get to the there that never arrives.

Be present.

This is yet another statement that is overflowing with judgment, because it seems the meaning has been hijacked by people seeking to create an unrealistic nirvana. A world where everyone is present, selfless, and only focused on the greater good of the world. Being present has taken on the baggage of a life engulfed in perpetual happiness. Being present has become a destination that is always just around the corner.

Where we spend our time matters. So often today, time spends us. The story above happens thousands of times a day, and at the center of the story is someone consumed with something other than where they are. There are enough people standing on a soapbox, yelling about what we must do to find happiness, be happy. My guess is, having read that sad, short story, you have already done a fine job judging and beating yourself up for not being present. Since what we focus on matters, where we spend our time matters, too. Why not try asking ourselves a few questions?

What if instead of being present, we asked the question, *Am I happy where I am spending my time right now?*

Then decide what to do.

-notes-

"The people I know...the people I have met...the people I will meet...the people I will never meet."

- Howard Behar, former president of Starbucks Coffee Company North America, Starbucks Coffee International and Author of
It's Not About The Coffee

-Gratitude is a Verb-

CHAPTER 14

PRACTICE #3 MOVE THROUGH FEAR

There is a common belief that people fear change. I think we fear thresholds.

Because walking through a threshold means a transition. It means giving something up, unlearning a long held belief, letting go of something comfortable, leaving behind thoughts, beliefs, and sometimes even friends. I think we fear letting go of what we know versus the thought of something new.

Fear is a choice.

I was standing in the doorway, looking back on a clear path, filled with thoughts and beliefs I was familiar with, unsure of what would happen if I walked through the door in front of me.

Fear is interesting.

It can be so strong it freezes me in my tracks, or so small I wave it off like a gnat. When I was five years old, I feared an imaginary monster under the bed. Now nearing 50, I fear being perceived as a naysayer in a meeting. No matter the age, fear is real for each of us. Today, most fear is based on perception or what we imagine might be.

Fear is a choice.

Sometimes I find myself running from my thoughts, hiding behind a forest of reasons or ducking in a cave of denial, just as my ancestors ran from their fears. The difference is my ancestors' fears were physical threats and a matter of life and death. In so many instances, I imagine threats to be real, when they are not.

The threats of today are different, but we can find ourselves reacting to them in the same way because of our brain. The brain is a powerful computer processor that takes in and catalogs information, experiences, images, and thoughts. Every time we have an experience or thought, it creates a path.

These paths become well worn and used often. Imagine being in a discussion with your spouse, and *that* topic comes up. Every couple has one. Your brain jumps to work and looks for a past experience or thought that is similar to the current one and files it. Do this over and over and a highway of values and norms are created that help make decisions and judgments based on past experience. This database and highway are so efficient that a similar past experience can trigger a response even without thinking.

Thoughts can trigger the fight or flight reaction. If your reaction to a situation in the past was, "Run!" your brain will continue to pull up this past experience and play it for you. It's as if there are hundreds of little workers running around in your head, and they get a few pieces of input from the current experience and say, "Oh, I've seen this one before," and run off to pull the tape from the past, complete with how you reacted and handled the situation.

When you began making a list of people you wanted to write to, did you second-guess yourself? It may have started with a series of questions like this: *What if they don't remember me? What will they think?* The thoughts then quickly transitioned into absolute statements, like, *They'll think I'm strange, or worse, stupid. I don't have time for this.* Each of these statements is tied to a past experience that you consider threatening.

You are not alone.

Second-guessing self-talk is natural and real. It originates from that part of the brain at the base of the skull, whose sole function is to help you survive physical and emotional threat, perceived or real. Without a conscious awareness that this exists, new ideas can quickly be squashed—rationalized away as ridiculous, impractical, or harebrained. If you questioned yourself, chances are this part of your brain has stepped in to protect you from fear. A fear that quite possibly has been lingering with you, tucked away in your subconscious from childhood experiences. Your efficient brain pulls fear tapes from the past like the fear of being rejected, fear of being laughed at, or maybe being the last one picked for the kickball team.

We all have them.

We give words power.

Words like *I can't, I should, I need to, I ought to*, are filled with judgment and are barriers to moving through fear. Each one of these words triggers emotions and fears that we have experienced in the past.

On day twenty-eight, one of my old experiences showed up without invitation when I called up my friend, Jess.

"I can't do this. I'm not going to make 50 letters in 50 days!"

"Well, hi. Why not?" Jess asked.

"Well, because I'm already behind."

"Behind what?"

"Behind!!" I yelled louder. "I'm not going to get all the letters written in time!" I was almost screaming into the phone, wondering why she wasn't as upset as I was. What kind of friend was she?!

"Well, didn't you make up the guidelines?"

"Yes."

"It's all invented. Do something different."

There was silence on the line as I shook my head and then laughed. "Oh, yeah. It is. It is all invented."

I was blinded by the two words "I can't" and allowed my fears to take over. Fear of failure, fear of not following through on a commitment, and the worst fear of all: fear of what people might think of me. I became so wrapped up in my fear that there was no room for creativity, new ideas, or an alternative solution.

Jess took the time to remind me that I had invented the rules, and I could change them whenever I wanted to. That's a concept we both learned several years ago from the book, *The Art of Possibility*, by Rosamund Stone Zander and Benjamin Zander. The Zanders' wisdom is refreshing.

When I decided to write 50 letters in 50 days, I decided without much thought that it would be 50 consecutive days. When I looked at it from a different perspective, I saw another solution. I decided to add two days of rest each week and give myself some breathing room. It worked! The small shift in perspective opened up space to continue to write letters and meet my goal of 50 in 50.

A small shift in perspective is sometimes all it takes.

The mind is powerful. Athletes use visualization as a way to see themselves being successful. I know it works. I used this technique for over a year when training for an international track and field competition. Every day I would imagine myself running around the track using all of my senses. I imagined feeling light on my feet, relaxed, and fluid. I imagined passing other participants with ease and finishing in first place in less than 21 minutes. I repeated this practice over and over, even on my worst training days. On the day of the race, my mind already knew what to do. I had run this race a thousand times in my head. As I crossed the finish line in first place I looked up at the clock, and it read 20:59. Twenty-one minutes.

In one of the best-known studies on creative visualization in sports, described in *Karate of Okinawa: Building Warrior Spirit*, by Robert Scaglione and William Cummins, Russian scientists compared four groups of Olympic athletes in terms of their training schedules:

Group 1 - 100% physical training

Group 2 - 75% physical training with 25% mental training

Group 3 - 50% physical training with 50% mental training

Group 4 - 25% physical training with 75% mental training

Group 4, with 75% of their time devoted to mental training performed the best.

The same technique can be used to move through fear. Take a look, as an observer, and acknowledge it exists. Then ask yourself, *What am I afraid of? What is the worst thing that could happen if I write this letter?*

Next, take a moment and remember the people you are grateful for. Using all of your senses, imagine them for a moment. Imagine them going to the mailbox, looking at the letter, and finding a spot to sit down. Imagine them opening the letter and beginning to read it. Imagine them holding the words you have written, smiling and hearing your voice as they savor the gift of words you have given them.

Take a moment and make a list of the words that describe the person you are writing to, and as you write each word, imagine moving through a threshold of gratitude.

... gratitude

-notes-

"While the pathway to love is not always evident, the pursuit of love is still worth it. Love, it's what really matters."

- Lakeesha Ransom, PhD Thought leader, Global Professor

-Gratitude is a Verb-

CONCLUSION
AN INVITATION

With pen in hand, begin writing, and you may find that words, which began as a memory, can flow through your heart, transferring your emotion to page. When your moments are replayed through the lens of gratitude, they can create an expansiveness that you will find spilling over into the rest of your day, and possibly life. When moments are called up again and reunited in the present, isn't the energy greater than it would be alone? Isn't that true about a lot of things in life? The whole is always greater than the sum of its parts.

Tucked away in the spine of this book, is my foundational belief that living a life of gratitude takes on lots of forms. You are the only one who can decide what gratitude looks like in your life.

Grab your life and get going.

Gratitude is a verb.

FINALLY: BIG THANKS

Thank you to a bunch of folks. The group who gave me the push to start writing: CWM, Lakeesha, Stacey, Jimmi, Jennifer, and Kristina. The first group of women who showed up to write a letter with me: Jess, Mardi, Kris, Shelly, Stacey, Cat, Darcy, Julie, Jodi, and Kendra. And to Dawn, Ginger, Jenny, and Jimmi—my writing friends, who always tell me the truth. My family and friends—you know who you are. Julie, who pushes me to be big. The folks at Best Buy— there are a bunch of you—who gave me a place to grow and dream and remember to live big. Emily the creative Guru who designed the cover. The folks at GoGreenhouse who believed in me from the beginning.

CPSIA information can be obtained at www.ICGtesting.com
Printed in the USA
BVOW072358261011

274561BV00004B/1/P